Written by : Alejandra Pozzo Stevenson
Illustrated by : Aniruddha Lele

Dear Parent,

Divorce is a difficult transition for every family member, but it is a necessary step towards happiness and peace for both mom and dad – which ultimately benefits the emotional well-being of your child.

This book was written to serve as a guide during this difficult transition as it sets new expectations and reminds your child that no matter what, they will always be loved by you.

As they adjust to this change, they may encounter feelings of sadness, guilt, and anger. My hope is that your love for them allows you to be patient, open, and kind as they cope with the loss of having both mom and dad together.

Much love,

Alejandra

ISBN: 978-1-954027-02-2 (paperback)

www.HappyHumanSociety.com

Made in the U.S.A.

To my nephew, may you always feel loved
in your two homes.

Mommy and Daddy
are getting a divorce.

At first, I didn't
know what that meant.

Mommy and Daddy will not live together anymore.

"You will have two homes now," they said.

My mommy has
her own house.

I have a room there that
we decorated together.

My daddy has his
own house, too.

So I have another room!
I helped Daddy put
that one together.

They got me this
special bag!

I get to carry my favorite things with me.

Some toys I leave at
Mommy's...

…and some I leave
at Daddy's.

Sometimes I miss my mommy, so Daddy calls her and she blows me kisses.

Sometimes I miss my daddy, so Mommy calls him and he says he misses me.

Then he makes me laugh!

Sometimes I feel sad and I want to cry.

Sometimes I feel angry and I want to SHOUT!

But no matter what I am feeling,

Mommy and Daddy always
help me figure it out.

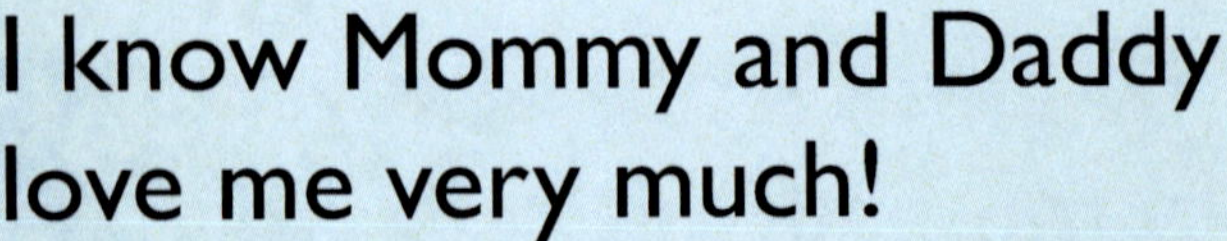
I know Mommy and Daddy
love me very much!

They moved apart,
but it wasn't because of me.

They said it was about grown-up stuff...

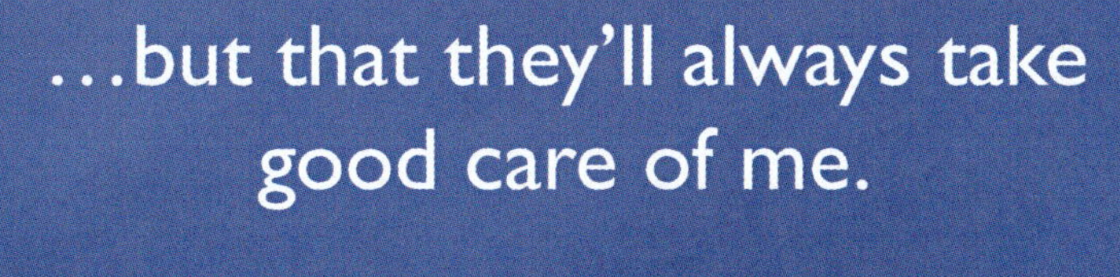

...but that they'll always take
good care of me.

Wherever I am,
they will ALWAYS love me!

And wherever they are,
I will ALWAYS love them!

Made in the USA
Middletown, DE
30 April 2024

53692029R00015